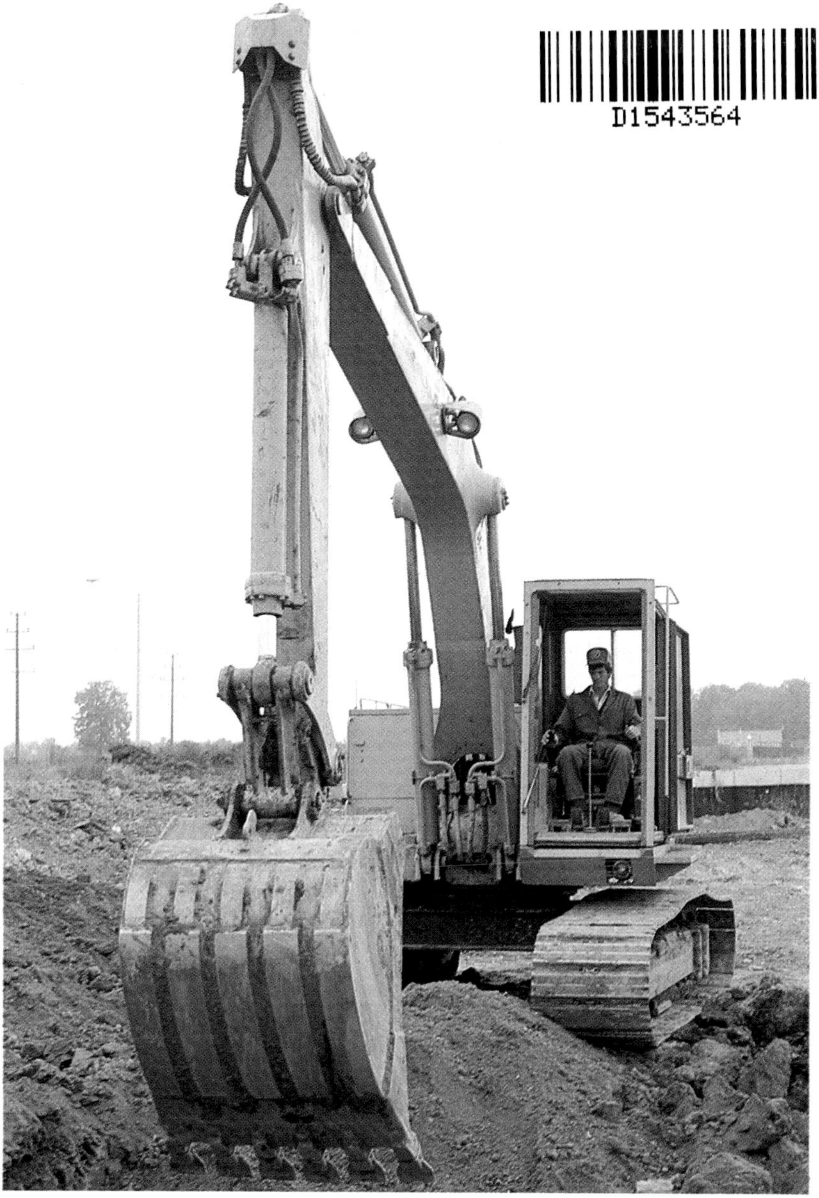

This machine digs.

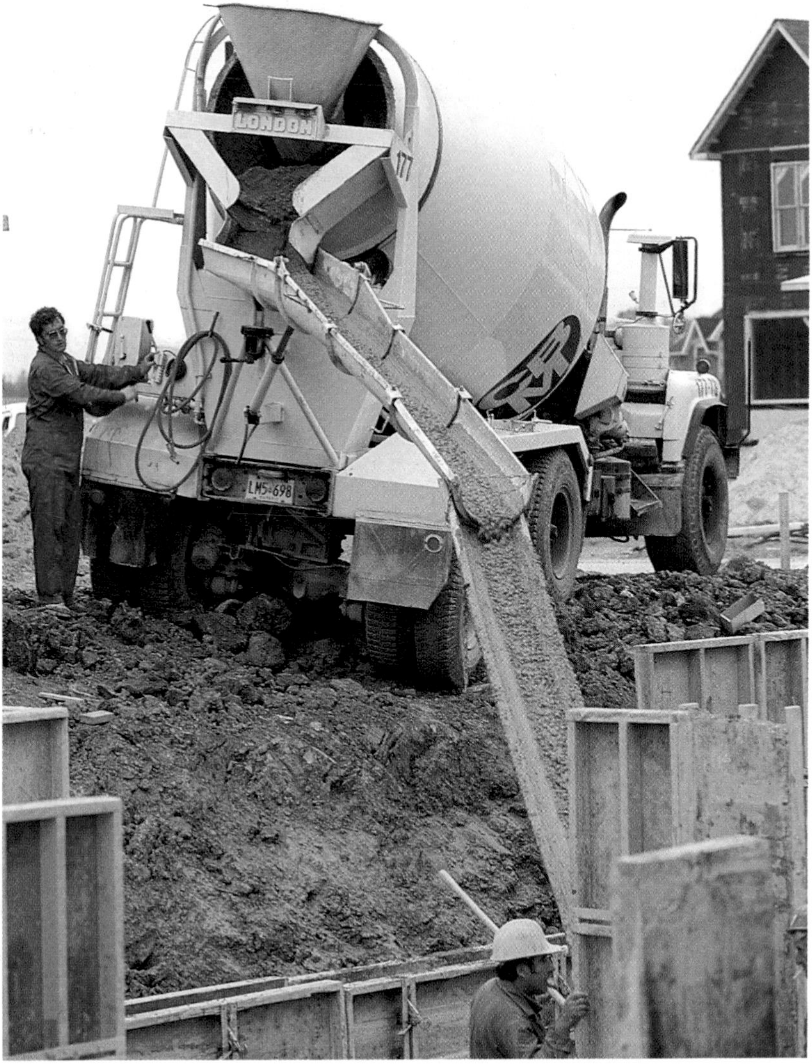

This machine pours.

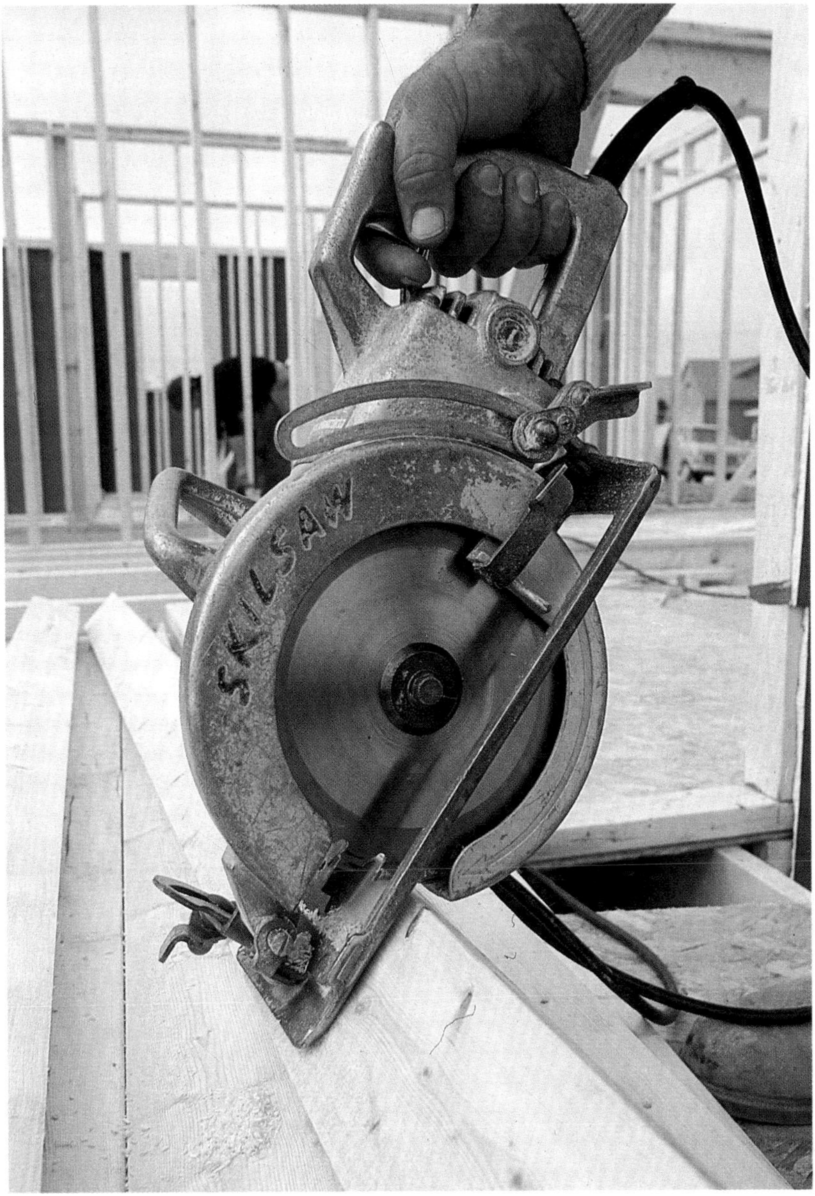

This machine saws.

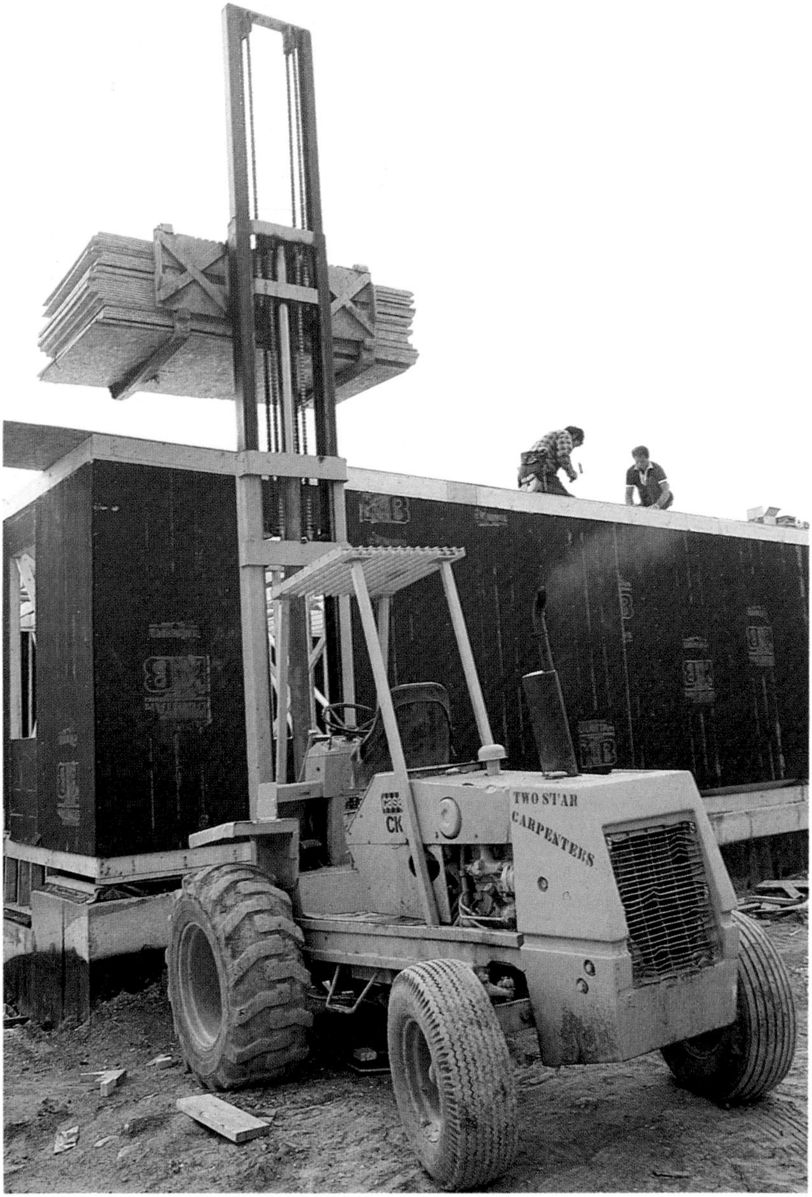

This machine lifts.

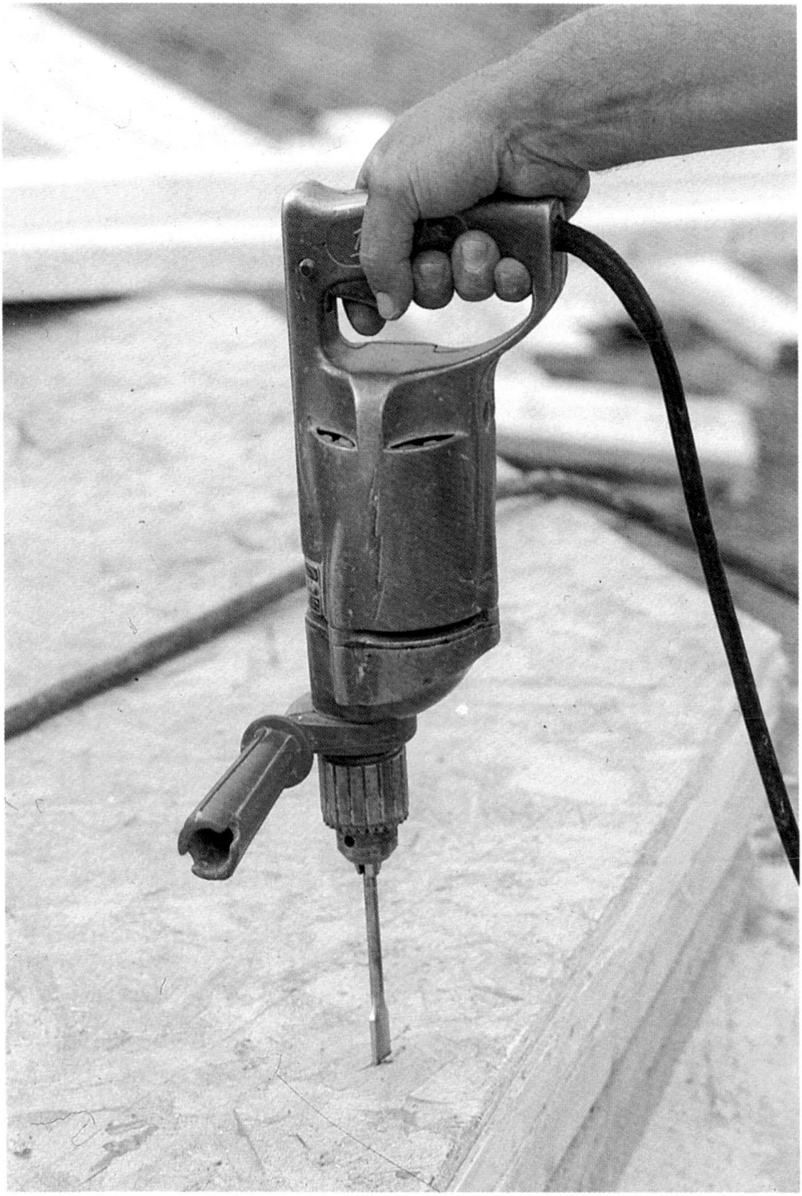

This machine drills.

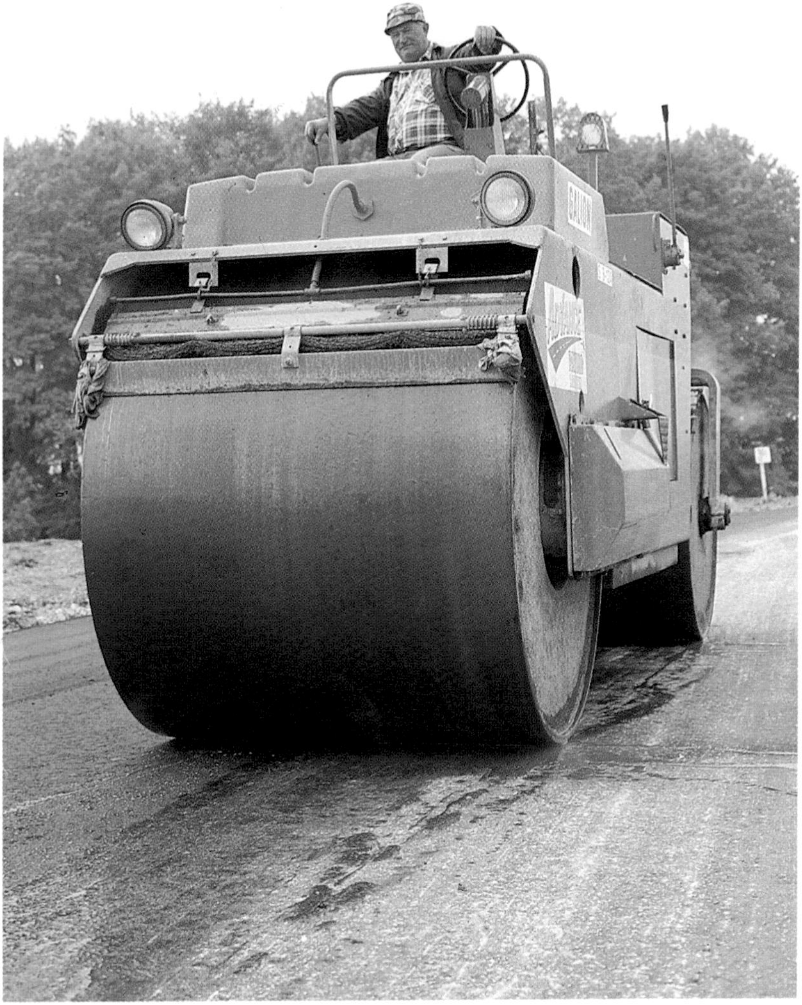

This machine rolls.

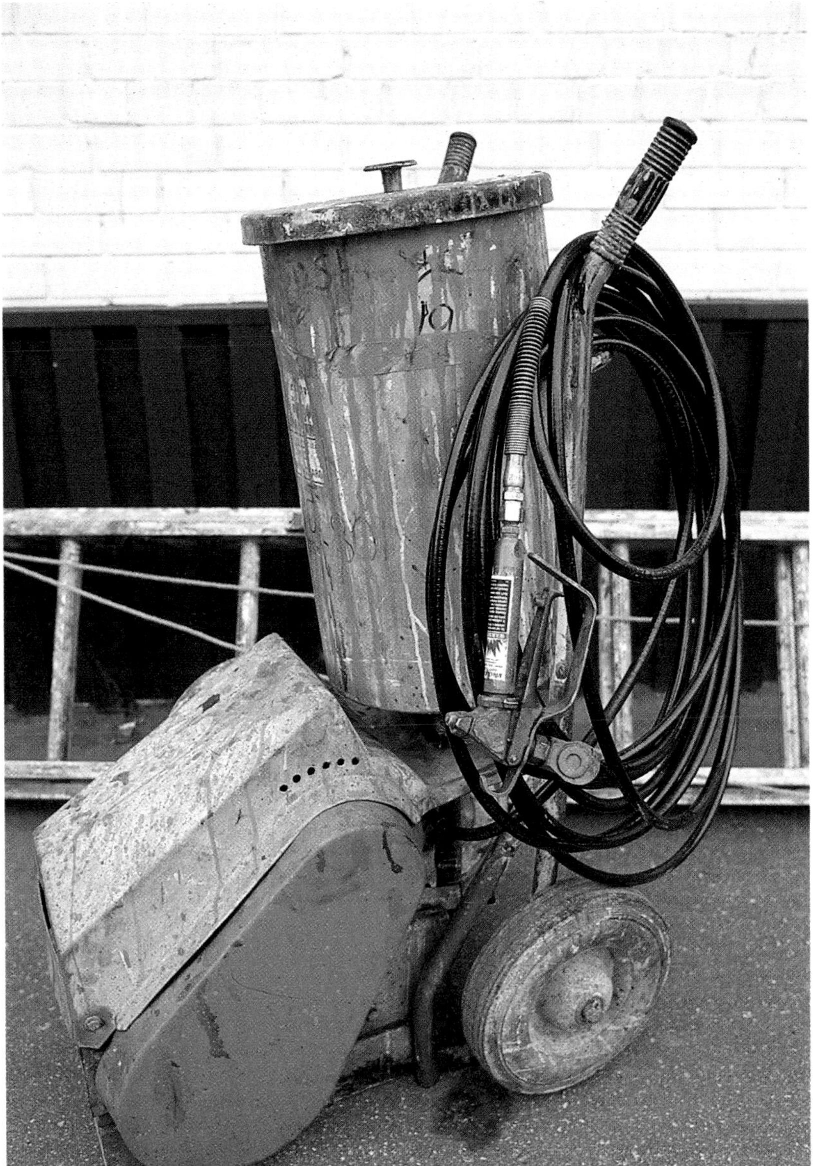

This machine paints.

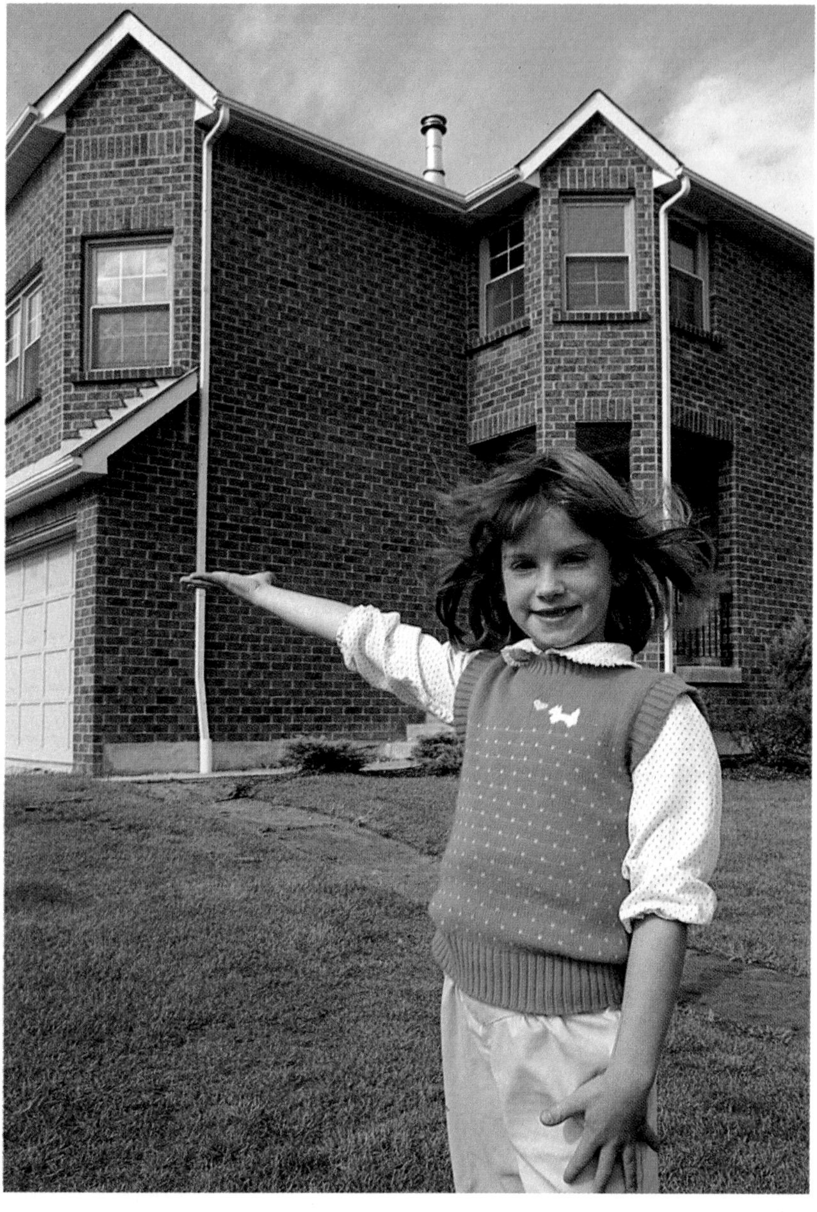

This is my new house.